WELCOME TO YOUR MIDLIFE CRISIS

Fortysomething ways to survive the ultimate rite of passage.

By Paul Della Valle

Illustrated by Lennie Peterson

C C C   P U B L I C A T I O N S

Published by

CCC Publications
1111 Rancho Conejo Blvd.
Suites 411 & 412
Newbury Park, CA 91320

Manufactured in the United States of America

Cover © 1996 CCC Publications

Interior illustrations © 1996 CCC Publications

Cover & interior art by Lennie Peterson

Cover/Interior production by Oasis Graphics

ISBN: 1-57644-000-1

If your local U.S. bookstore is out of stock, copies of this book may be obtained by mailing check or money order for $5.95 per book (plus $2.50 to cover postage and handling) to: CCC Publications; 1111 Rancho Conejo Blvd.; Suites 411 & 412; Newbury Park, CA 91320

Pre-publication Edition – 1/96

First printing – 7/96

DEDICATION

**We dedicate this book
to our families
and to
midlifers everywhere.**

INTRODUCTION

Middle age is the time when a man is always thinking that in a week or two, he will feel as good as ever.
— Don Marquis

Welcome to your midlife crisis.

The truth is, of course, that you will never feel as good as ever again. The truth is from here on in you'll just get older, uglier, weaker, slower, sicker and fatter.

Did we forget anything?

Oh yeah, your days as a sex object are, ah, petering out. Definitely petering out and in rapid decline.

In fact, it's all downhill from here.

No doubt, you hoped it was just a touch of the flu — the aches and pains, the general malaise that begins when you wake up and stays most of the day.

A touch of the flu doesn't last several years though. Face it, you're actually having a full-blown midlife crisis.

The signs are ubiquitous. The lines around your eyes are looking more and more like a road map of Harvard Square. If you are a fortysomething woman, the only time you turn heads now is when you are walking with your teenage daughter. If you are a fortysomething man, the hairs in your nose are growing thicker than the hairs on your head. Young women who use to flirt back are calling you "Sir."

Or they're calling the police.

"Hey Jennifer, there's some old guy out here drooling and leering at me."

It's rough getting into that fifth decade. Rough.

You tell your friends you want to have just one more good year playing softball before hanging up the cleats and they say "What do you mean one more?" You look into the mirror and see your mother. Not good, especially if you're a man.

You go to bed tired. You wake up tired. You work tired. You're so tired that you're too tired to recognize you're tired. Then you get cranky. A hangover lasts a week — minimum. PMS lasts 26 or so days every month, and winters last forever. Dance all night? You're not even sure you could make it through the six-minute version of "Shout" these days. You look at Playboy magazine and realize the bodacious centerfold is closer in age to your son than she is to you.

A lot closer.

Sooner or later, a 21-year-old office clerk will ask you who sang "Yesterday."

Suddenly, you won't be half as young as you used to be.

Of course, you're not alone. There's a whole bunch of us out there who are hitting 40 or fortysomething. We are all wondering what happened to our youth and reluctantly conceding that we will probably never:

(A) Write the great American novel,

(B) Score the winning goal in the Stanley Cup playoffs or,

(C) If you're a woman, fit into one of those Victoria's Secret butt floss bikinis; or, if you're guy, fit into one of those potato-in-the-front bikinis that French Canadian guys wear on beaches in Florida and Maine. (Of course those French Canadian guys don't fit in their suits either, but c'est la vie, as they say in Montreal.)

In his book, The Seasons of a Man's Life, former Yale psychologist Daniel J. Levinson estimated 70 percent of the people between the ages of 40 and 45 experience some sort of midlife crisis.

That means if 10 of us baby-boomers are in the same room, seven of us are totally bonkers, cheating on our spouses, planning to buy a sports car or thinking about quitting our jobs and opening a gourmet restaurant in Kennebunkport, Maine.

This is not good.

And it's just going to get worse. Luckily for us, though, hitting the Big 4-0 or even the Big 4-5 doesn't mean you're quite ready for adult diapers. Nope, you still have a couple of good years left. And look at it this way — no matter how you screw up in the next few years you can always blame it on your midlife crisis.

So go for it. Here are fortysomething sure-fire ways to not only survive, but thrive, in your autumn years.

Welcome to your midlife crisis.

1. GROW A PONY TAIL

QUESTION: What looks more pathetic than a fortysomething guy with one of those skinny little pony tails?

ANSWER: Nothing.

2. WEAR MINISKIRTS

The fortysomething female version of the aging male ponytail is the midlife miniskirt. We have just two words of caution for women contemplating buying one:

1. Cellulite.
2. Gravity.

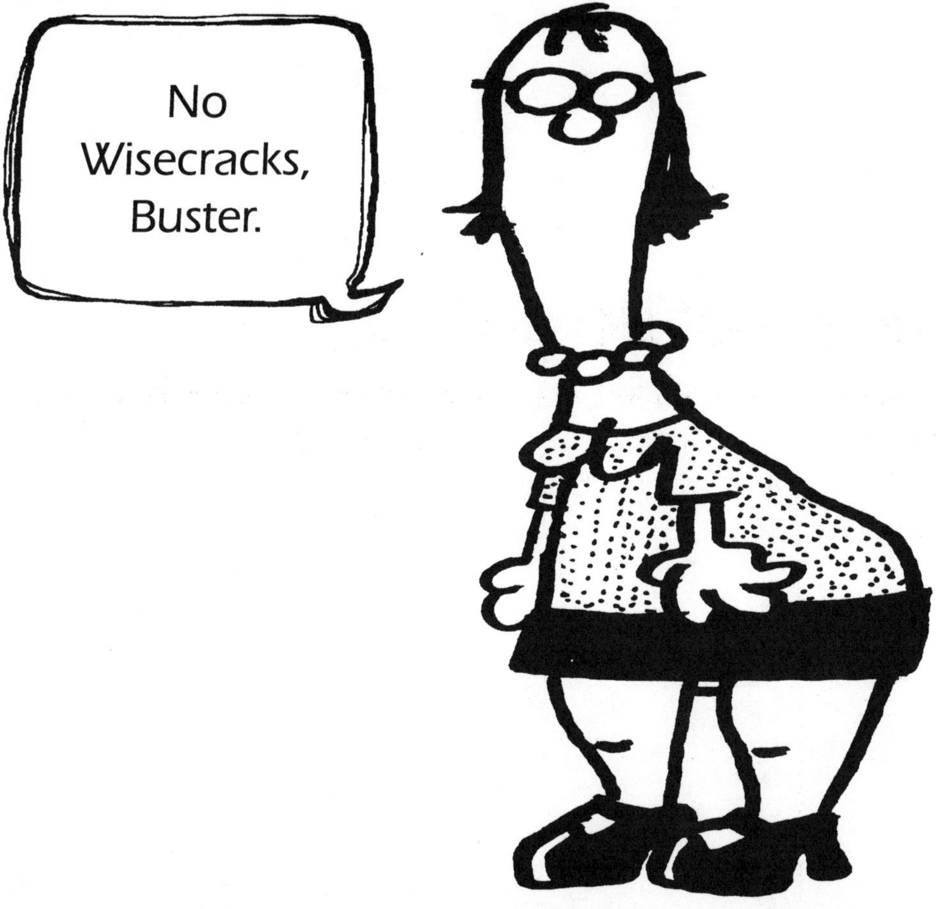
No Wisecracks, Buster.

3. SEE A SHRINK

Talk about all the great issues that are bothering you, specifically your unfulfilled life and upcoming death.

Wake him up when your half-hour is over.

Pay him 100 bucks.

4. SHRINK

No, we are not st-st-stuttering. This time we are using the word "shrink" quite literally. And if you think you get no respect now, just wait till you're a 5-foot-2-inch geezer.

It is a medical fact that, not only have you stopped growing, but you may soon start to shrink. This has something to do with gravity and your bones being compressed and it happens to just about everybody — when they get real, real old.

Which, in your case, will be next year.

5. GET SERIOUS ABOUT GOLF

Becoming preoccupied by a time-consuming, frustrating and extremely expensive game is one way to fill in the time between your long-lost youth and your approaching geezer-hood. Resist the urge to do this.

Nothing, other than a pony tail on a fortysomething guy, is quite so pathetic as a flock of fortysomething guys standing in the rain on the sixth tee of a public course at 6:30 on a Saturday morning, every one of them wearing little plastic raincoats and bright red knickers, and every one of them telling their friends, "My boss's new secretary has a great ass" or "I can't wait till I'm 49 so I can shoot my age for nine holes."

Actually, that is even more pathetic than a pony tail.

6. CHANGE SUBSCRIPTIONS

It is the natural way of things that you will in the next decade stop subscribing to Cosmopolitan ("How to please your man in bed") and start subscribing to Modern Maturity magazine ("How to cash his 401K when your man drops dead"). To ease this transition, you may now want to make the big catalogue switch first — from Victoria's Secret to L.L. Bean. Face it, your peek-a-boo lace bra and butt-floss panties days are behind you. You will never look like those perky Victoria's Secret models again — if you ever did. You are entering the plaid and flannel years. You cannot turn back.

7. HAIR TODAY, GONE TOMORROW

Pluck the gray hairs now growing in your sideburns.

Pluck the gray hairs now growing in your nose.

Pluck the gray hairs now growing from your ears.

Paste them all on that rapidly enlarging shiny spot on the top of your head.

8. BUY A RUG

Hey, buddy, so what if you're getting a little, er, thin on top? Women love follically challenged guys —think of babe magnets Yul Brynner and Mr. T and Elmer Fudd.

Actually, forget about Mr. Fudd. Obviously, baldness isn't for everyone.

If it isn't for you, you do have options.

For instance, you could cut and paste the tresses growing out of your ears onto your head (See No. 7). Or you could join a hair association and let some "doctor" sew someone else's pompadour into your skull.

Or, you could just buy a toupee. No muss, no fuss. And rugs today aren't like that dead rodent your 10th grade math teacher used to wear on his head.

Nope, they look great nowadays. No one will know. And, really, those people aren't laughing at you behind your back. Really.

9. GROW WEIRD FACIAL THINGS

You will soon begin to grow weird warts and moles on your face.

It's cool. Actor Robert DiNero has a mole. Supermodel Cindy Crawford has a mole. You will too.

Then you'll have two. Then you'll have three.

And just wait till those liver spots start appearing on your hands.

Very, very sexy.

10. ADJUST TO MIDLIFE SEX

About the time you hit fortysomething, your husband may have a bout with impotence. This can occur for three reasons:

1: Maybe he has performance anxiety.
2. Maybe he had too many beers with his lunch.
3. Maybe you forgot to shut off the lights before you took your clothes off.

11. HAVE AN AFFAIR WITH A YOUNGER WOMAN

This is standard midlife crisis stuff for men, often as a result of the aforementioned marital bed problems. Of course, when the fine young thing says, "Oooh, that was wonderful, big daddy, let's do it again," you might have a little problem in the ol' satisfying department. And don't confess to your wife after the nubile babe moves on to some five-times-a-night 25-year-old stockbroker. If you do, read No. 13 immediately.

12. DO A YOUNG STUD

As many women turn fortysomething and go into full-blown midlife crisis, they will start to increasingly notice the tight buns on UPS drivers, landscapers and their daughter's boyfriends. They then develop a desire to - how shall we say it tactfully? - do some young stud in the Mot O' Lodge out on the edge of town.

Even if said young stud is available, you should resist acting on this desire because the following two things will probably happen:

1. Aforementioned young stud will charge you money.

2. Aforementioned young stud will innocently say something like "Gee, Mrs. Smith, I wonder if Danielle's boobs are going to sag like yours when she gets old."

13. GO THROUGH THE BIG D

Nothing typifies the midlife crisis so much as the divorce. And getting one is a lot easier than some people think. Here's how: If you don't mind living in a one-room apartment and being broke all the time, just let your wife catch you in the sack with that pretty young receptionist from your office. (Or, if you're a woman, just get caught, ah, entertaining the bronze young Adonis from the landscaping crew on the day your husband decides to come home from the office early).

Heck, you'll be divorced in practically no time at all. And just wait till the judge hears you explain your fling with Ms. Nubile 19-Going-On-20. "Your honor, I was having a midlife crisis and ..."

Go directly to the poorhouse. Do not pass Go. Do not receive any paychecks. Do not touch those co-signed bank accounts.

14. CHANGE CAREERS

So what if you've been making 80K a year as an accountant? Wouldn't it be more fulfilling to quit and become a folk singer?

Get that old guitar out of the closet, buy a Mel Bay book and learn how to form a G chord. Practice a month, then give the boss your notice.

Carpe Diem. Go for it.

Why not? Pass-the-hat coffeehouses in Unitarian churches pay really well. And if you don't have a guitar you can always buy one cheap from a fortysomething folk singer who has decided to chuck it all and fulfill his lifelong dream of becoming a CPA.

15. BECOME A VEGETARIAN

Many people become vegetarians when they hit their midlife crisis.

The fortysomething female generally gives up meat because she decides to live a more healthy lifestyle, and also because she secretly hopes to look more like the slender young woman who works in the health food store.

The fortysomething male who becomes a vegetarian usually has a multitude of reasons:

The first is that his doctor tells him he is now walking around with about 6.2 pounds of undigested sausage and hamburger in his colon.

The second is he learns his cholesterol level has actually topped Joe DiMaggio's lifetime batting average.

The third reason a man becomes a vegetarian is that, while on an errand picking up tofu for his wife, he is told by the slender young woman who works in the health food store that he should give up meat because he'll live longer and feel healthier and look better.

The fourth is that he notices the slender young woman who works in the health food store has a great ass.

16. BUY THE CORVETTE

Many a male midlife crisis survivor has lived through a crash in a shiny red sports car shaped like a dick. This is because he bought the shiny red sports car figuring it would make him appear younger and hipper and more attractive, and that the slender young woman with the great ass who works in the health food store would thus jump into the front seat and cozy up to him like a kitten when he offered her a ride home.

What happens instead is the slender young woman with the great ass leaves the health store with a crunchy granola type — a young crunchy granola type — in a VW bus. So our hero goes into full-blown midlife crisis, drives the aforementioned shiny red sports phallic symbol (a used Monte Carlo can be substituted for the 'Vette if money is an issue) to a bar, drinks six scotches and picks up some aging, drunk barfly. Drunk flyperson then gets her girdle stuck in the steering wheel while attempting a mobile love-a-thon, thus causing our hero to crash into a tree.

Aging hooker's girdle is generally introduced as "Exhibit A" in both her lawsuit and the ensuing divorce trial, thus making our midlife hero's lawyer extremely anxious to settle both.

17. GO TO JAIL

Many in-crisis fortysomething males discover their divorces cost so much that they aren't able to scrape up bail or afford adequate legal representation when their own up-close-and-personal drunk flyperson/Corvette case is adjudicated.

That often means spending a few nights or weeks in the hoosegow. We're talking a real midlife crisis now, and it could happen to you. If it does, here's a couple of hints to help make your stay behind bars more comfortable:

If you find some candy on your cot when you come back from the exercise yard, don't eat it. And ask the screw to lock your cell door real tight, or you might get a surprise midnight visit from Bruno. Bruno is large and Bruno is lonely. Can you squeal like a pig for Bruno? Sure you can.

18. BUTT OUT

Look at it this way, ladies: If God didn't want women's butts to grow a bit bigger in middle age, He wouldn't have invented Dove Bars and relaxed-fit jeans.

Enjoy your enhanced back porch — heck, just think of the money you'll save on bleacher cushions if you go to the Indy 500 next year.

Consider buying one of those Buns O' Steel exercise machines only if your bum gets really humongous. A good indication that has occurred is if you go swimming in the ocean and the captains of two or more passing whale-watching boats point to you and shout, "Thar she blows!"

19. LOWER YOUR EXPECTATIONS

You didn't really want to make senior vice president. Nope, too much pressure. Yep, assistant stockroom clerk on the 3-to-11 shift is just fine. Yes sir, who wants a good-looking secretary and a key to the executive washroom. Not me. Nope, I'm just happy to be down here with the boys, sir. Just happy to have any job at my age.

20. BEND OVER AND SPREAD 'EM

One benefit of turning 40, if you're a guy, is that at the end of every annual physical from now on, your doctor will slip a glove onto his right hand and give you a prostate exam.

We're talking up close ...

And extremely, ouch, personal.

21. BEGIN THE GREAT COVERUP

About 126 million women now live in the United States. Some, upon turning fortysomething, will graciously accept the wrinkles on their faces, referring to them as laugh lines or signs of the wisdom and experience they've gained at midlife.

The other 125,999,995, of course, will totally freak out and start laminating their countenances with all sorts of concealers and mascaras and eye shadows and eye liners and make-up. This is OK — many young studs have had summer jobs painting houses and are turned on by the smell of oil-based products.

Just don't go overboard. More than, say, one-half inch of make-up will make you look like the Bride of Frankenstein — or worse, like Tammy Faye Bakker — and scare off potential afternoon sex partners.

22. TAKE UP COUNTRY LINE DANCING

Gosh, almighty, Li'l Darlin', that-thar boogie for the creatively impaired we been watching on TNN sure looks like a heck of a lot of fun. What say, we buy us some of them-thar lizard skin boots, a couple of big ol' 10-gallon hats, two pairs of them straight-legged jeans (with just a scosh more room in the butt of yours, of course) and matching cowboy shirts? Then we can promenade on down to the local Elks club on Friday night and learn to boot-scoot and boogie and tush push and, and , and, heck, we'll be just about everything we figured was totally geeky back in high school.

23. LOOK ON THE BRIGHT SIDE OF THE CHANGE 'O LIFE

Many fortysomething women in midlife crisis fear the onset of menopause. There is no reason for this. Sure you might sweat a bit more in some places, and get a little dry now and then in certain other places. But just think of the money you'll save on tampons and birth control pills in the years you have left. And just think of how nice those hot flashes will feel when you're out sledding on a cold winter day.

Best of all, menopause gives you a good excuse to wear purple and act totally bonkers every day for the next five years.

24. GO THE OTHER WAY

Female bisexuality is in. Many women in midlife crisis are looking deep within themselves and deciding that their husbands are the real reason they are getting old and wrinkled. They decide then to become lesbians. They cut their hair real short, dye it blonde, get their upper ears and noses and nipples and navels pierced, and leave their husbands and children. They then take up with other women who have cut and dyed their hair and got pierced in a zillion different places.

The vast majority of these nouveau lesbian couples open art galleries or trendy little restaurants in Northhampton, Mass. Some of these couples still get old and wrinkled. Some don't, because all those earrings lock up while they're performing unfamiliar sex acts and they are found weeks, or even months, later in embarrassing positions.

25. CONTROL YOUR DRINKING

Many people in full-blown midlife crisis become concerned about their alcohol intake. That is because what used to be a couple of glasses of beers on that special weekend night out has now become a few carafes of white wine during lunch, a six-pack any time the 49ers are on television, or a couple of martinis before every meal.

Not to worry. Many midlifers get rid of all their unhealthy guilt feelings by pledging to drink only on special occasions.

"Here's a toast to sunrise."

"Here's a toast to Barney the Dinosaur."

"Here's a toast to, uh, 10:33 a.m."

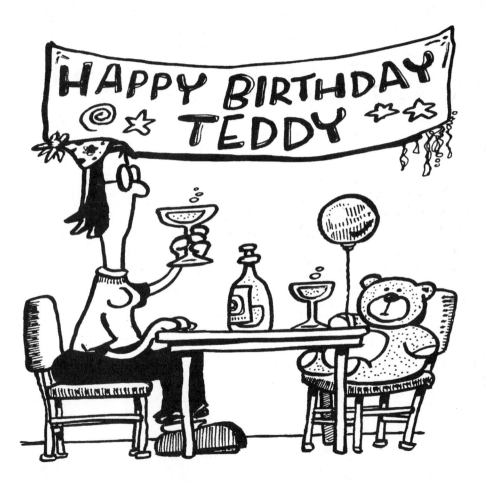

26. BE WILLFUL

Making out a will can trigger a midlife crisis. For many it is the ultimate acknowledgement that they have probably passed the halfway post and could drop dead at any (gasp) second.

This is understandable. After all, a will is a very strange thing. You have to decide who you're going to give all your stuff to when you die, even though you're still alive, which gives all your beneficiaries time to screw you over. Like, you could make out your will and give all your stuff to your wife and then she could turn around and pay her hunka-hunka-burning-love boyfriend to accidentally run you over with your own riding lawnmower.

But remember, making out your midlife will can be fun too. Try this in yours:

"I bequeath all my stock in IBM to Phoebe Asstodyfo."

Of course, you never did own any stock in IBM and you never actually did do anyone named Phoebe Asstodyfo. But all those greedy relatives of yours sitting in the lawyer's office won't know that.

27. REDISCOVER SEX, DRUGS and ROCK' N' ROLL

There's just no better cure for a midlife crisis than going to an outdoor Lollapalooza concert and smoking a few joints. "Like, uh, wow, man, I'm flashing back to my youth, all these half-naked hippie girls twirling around, the driving music and loud grooving."

So what if you and your lawn chair will stand out like that guy with the crewcut cleaning the portable toilets at Woodstock? So what if you'll suddenly notice a large and visibly paranoid segment of the audience looking at you, and then someone will shout "NARC!" and dozens of stronger-than-they-look heavy metal dudes will start beating the living crap out of you, even as your young date takes off her top and starts rolling around in the mud with some long-haired kid who turns out to be your son?

28. WORK ON THOSE BUNS O' STEEL

Here's a great money saving tip which may come in handy when you're trying to figure out how to pay young Buffy's annual $28,000 tuition bill from the local community college.

Everyone who has ever had a midlife crisis — that is to say everyone who has ever reached fortysomething — has decided what he or she really needs is to get more exercise. And almost everyone of those born-again Jack LaLane's has gone down to the local department store and bought a bran' spankin' new stationary bicycle, or a rowing machine, or a combination rowing machine/stationary bike/ tummy flattener/bum hardener.

Studies now show, however, that less than 1 percent of those millions of machines are ever actually used more than once. So don't buy one of them new. Just go to any yard sale and look for a woman who weighs between 180 and 240 pounds and is wearing a money apron.

Guaranteed she'll have a stationary bike for sale.

Guaranteed it will have less than 30 miles on the odometer.

Guaranteed it will have less than 60 miles on the odometer when you sell it at your yard sale next spring.

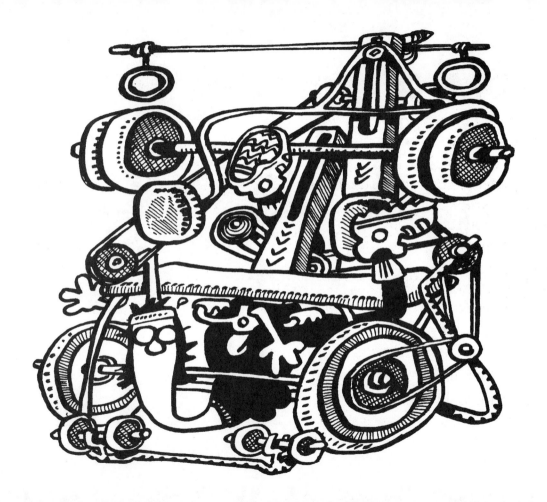

29. ACCEPT BEING ONCE-A-WEEKERS

Remember how you and your spouse used to be young and make love about a gazillion times a day? Remember how you always joked about getting old and becoming once-a-weekers?

Well, Tuesdays are pretty darn special now, aren't they?

The bad news is you'll probably soon be once-a-monthers.

And then it's just going to get worse.

30. GET AN EARRING

Some men are overcome in midlife with the desire to get an ear pierced. This occurs approximately three times as often as the corresponding female midlife desire to get a butterfly tattooed onto a cellulite-covered butt cheek. We caution against both of these body-altering procedures for some obvious and not so obvious reasons.

Those of you fortysomething guys who are thinking about getting an earring might want to consider that if you get your right ear pierced — or is it the left? — you just might be making a statement you don't really want to make.

Or maybe you do? Hey, big fella, that's up to you.

However, if you simply hope getting an earring will make you appear younger and hipper, we urge you to get two others things instead:

1. Real.
2. A life.

31. STOP PICKING UP BABIES

Relax, there is a grand scheme to all of this.

Consider that just about the time your Change O' Life baby is big enough to stop demanding "Mommy, Mommy, pick me up," your back is going to be far too weak to pick up anything at all, let alone a squirming 40 pounds of toddler.

The same neat equation works for your impending and unavoidable midlife memory loss.

It's like, uh, what were we saying?

Oh yeah, midlife memory loss. Just about the time you start getting your teenage children's names confused whenever you attempt to speak to one of them — "Bob, uh, Joe, uh, Jim, uh, Samantha" — none of them will want to talk to you anymore anyway.

Trust us, it all works out.

32. SAY GOODBYE TO YOUR TOES

The beer belly is to men what the big ol' Dove Bar butt is to women. No one is absolutely sure why this is so. Some theorists think this gender-oriented difference has something to do with the way prehistoric people stored body fat. Others believe it has more to do with bowling.

In any case, as a fortysomething male you should graciously accept the basketball-like protuberance that has started to grow below your sunken chest and will soon overlap your increasingly flaccid wee-wee. Wear that gut proudly — there is simply no realistic way to get rid of it.

Well, actually there is one way to get rid of it. You could give up beer.

OK, like we said, there is simply no realistic way to get rid of it.

33. BECOME YOUR PARENTS

Pop quiz time:

Did your parents ever seem young to you when you were a kid?

Did you ever think your parents were hip? Or cool?

Did you ever think your parents actually *did* it or would have any desire to *do* it after you and your brothers and sisters were born?

Now, look in the mirror. Try to look at yourself as your kids look at you.

Recognize anyone?

ARRRRRRRRRRRGGHH......

34. BUY A CEMETERY PLOT

First the good news: Everyone is going to need one sooner or later.

Now the bad news: You're closer to the sooner side.

And it's getting sooner every day.

35. READ THE OBITUARIES

While we're on the subject of your rapidly approaching demise, no doubt you have started seriously scanning the obituary pages in your local daily newspaper. You didn't do that when you were 20 or 30 or 35, did you?

And, no doubt redux, you have probably started playing the There-Must-Have-Been-A-Reason-He/She-Died-So-Young game, like "Oh yeah, he had a genetic disease" or "You can tell by the contributions request she used drugs" or "Obviously, anyone that heavy wasn't going to live to see 55" or ....

36. TAKE UP A NEW SPORT

Co-ed softball getting a little too rough for you, Bunky? Well, don't despair. Golf is not the only sport you'll be able to play in the coming years. Heck, many people bowl well into their 50s. And the national champs in croquet, horseshoes and tiddlywinks are almost always geezers, that is to say, people even older than you.

Just think, if you start playing shuffleboard now, you'll be real good at it by the time your kids ship you off to the Happy Acres Retirement Home in a couple of decades. And you know how those old broads go for a guy who can handle a, er, one of those things you push the shuffleboard pucks with.

Don't come a knockin' if the wheelchair's a rockin', sonny.

37. BUY EYEGLASSES

No, the type on this page didn't just get smaller. Hey, you're fortysomething and you need glasses. It was inevitable.

38. LIVE VICARIOUSLY THROUGH YOUR CHILDREN

Remember, the key word here is vicariously.

Gentlemen, resist the temptation to join in any backyard sporting event that involves teenagers and footballs, even Nerf footballs.

There are three reasons why you should not attempt to recreate your foregone days of gridiron glory:

1. Teenage boys are young and strong and fast and flexible. You are old and weak and slow and brittle.

2. You will be knocked down and you will be unable to get up.

3. The crack of your butt will appear above your underwear as you attempt to run and this will deeply embarrass your son.

Actually, your mere presence will deeply embarrass your son.

39. DYE YOUR HAIR

Oh yeah, no one will notice when the ol' Silver Fox shows up at work with jet black locks.

Really, no one will notice.

Just make sure you keep your pants on at the next office party.

40. ACCEPT PAIN

Yes, maybe you did strain your neck because you sneezed particularly hard — *and* farted — just as you reached for that laxative in the cupboard.

And, maybe, if you had just warmed up a little you wouldn't have pulled a hamstring playing basketball in the driveway with your son.

And, yes, it is possible that 25-pound bag of dog chow was somehow heavier this time, and that's why you sprained your back in the grocery store parking lot and had to miss work for a week.

The bottom line, though, is that all sorts of physical things that use to be a snap for you to do are now causing grievous injury and lingering pain.

Accept this. Your body is breaking down as surely as night follows day. You are in the twilight of mobility. Arthritis, osteoporosis and tendinitis will follow. Pretty soon just about every movement you make will hurt.

Like hell. And for a long time.

41. BUY MATCHING OUTFITS

The wearing of identical outfits is the first sure signal that you and your significant other have survived your midlife crisis and accepted that your youth is gone forever.

This defining moment might occur when you go off for an evening of the aforementioned country line dancing in matching ten-gallon hats.

It might occur when you buy "He" and "She" plaid knickers in the pro shop at the local golf course. It might occur when you go on a second honeymoon to the Bahamas and don matching tropical print shirts "just for fun."

You cannot be certain when this will happen, only that it will.

And, gee, won't you two make a pair?

42. APPRECIATE THE MIDLIFE POSITIVES

Yes, you are getting older.

Your body is slowly breaking down. No one thinks you're sexy at all anymore, and your kids think you're incredibly out of touch.

The good news, though, is that you can finally relax.

Your midlife crisis will soon be over.

You made it. Give yourself a hand — even if there are liver spots all over it. At least you'll never have to pretend to be hip again. And you'll never ever have to watch another minute of MTV.

Your best years await.

Wear your wrinkled bowling shirts and support hose proudly. Get rid of that little sports car and buy a big ol' Caddy to cart your big ol' butt all over town. Feel free to pass gas in front of your family. More good news, in less than a decade, you'll qualify for the coveted American Association of Retired Persons senior discount card.

But the best news of all is that neither you nor your mate will ever have to worry again about the other running off with someone else.

Hey, no offense, but just look at each other.

Ain't life grand?

PAUL DELLA VALLE was named 1993 Humor Columnist of the Year by the New England Press Association and has been voted Columnist of the Year for the last five years by the people of Worcester, MA, which is New England's second largest city and a community in the throes of its own midlife crisis. Della Valle is the author of *My Favorite Column of Yours is the One Your Wife Wrote*, a collection of his essays. He is also a contributing editor of *Worcester Magazine*, a singer-songwriter and a teacher of writing and journalism at Clark University in Worcester and at Northeastern University in Boston. He lives with his wife and children in Lancaster, MA.

LENNIE PETERSON's dynamic and diverse artwork has been featured in books, magazines, puzzles, games, advertisements and promotions, as well as on album and book covers distributed nationally and abroad. His children's books, in affiliation with the television series *Ghostwriter*, are available in bookstores everywhere. His self-syndicated weekly comic strip *The Big Picture* appears in newspapers and magazines around the country. His award-winning pen and ink surrealisms are featured in galleries in New York and throughout New England. Peterson is a former assistant professor at Berklee College of Music. He currently plays trombone with the Clutch Grabwell band. The band's debut CD was released to rave reviews in May, 1995. Peterson lives in Worcester, MA.

TITLES BY CCC PUBLICATIONS

Retail $4.99

"?" book
POSITIVELY PREGNANT
WHY MEN ARE CLUELESS
CAN SEX IMPROVE YOUR GOLF?
THE COMPLETE BOOGER BOOK
FLYING FUNNIES
MARITAL BLISS & OXYMORONS
THE VERY VERY SEXY ADULT DOT-TO-DOT BOOK
THE DEFINITIVE FART BOOK
THE COMPLETE WIMP'S GUIDE TO SEX
THE CAT OWNER'S SHAPE UP MANUAL
PMS CRAZED: TOUCH ME AND I'LL KILL YOU!
RETIRED: LET THE GAMES BEGIN
THE OFFICE FROM HELL
FOOD & SEX
FITNESS FANATICS
YOUNGER MEN ARE BETTER THAN RETIN-A
BUT OSSIFER, IT'S NOT MY FAULT

Retail $4.95

YOU KNOW YOU'RE AN OLD FART WHEN...
1001 WAYS TO PROCRASTINATE
HORMONES FROM HELL II
SHARING THE ROAD WITH IDIOTS
THE GREATEST ANSWERING MACHINE MESSAGES
    OF ALL TIME
WHAT DO WE DO NOW?? (A Guide For New Parents)
HOW TO TALK YOU WAY OUT OF A TRAFFIC TICKET
THE BOTTOM HALF (How To Spot Incompetent
    Professionals)
LIFE'S MOST EMBARRASSING MOMENTS
HOW TO ENTERTAIN PEOPLE YOU HATE
YOUR GUIDE TO CORPORATE SURVIVAL
THE SUPERIOR PERSON'S GUIDE TO EVERYDAY
    IRRITATIONS
GIFTING RIGHT

Retail $5.95

LOVE DAT CAT
CRINKLED 'N' WRINKLED
SIGNS YOU'RE A GOLF ADDICT
SMART COMEBACKS FOR STUPID QUESTIONS
YIKES! IT'S ANOTHER BIRTHDAY
SEX IS A GAME
SEX AND YOUR STARS
SIGNS YOUR SEX LIFE IS DEAD
40 AND HOLDING YOUR OWN
50 AND HOLDING YOUR OWN
MALE BASHING: WOMEN'S FAVORITE PASTIME
THINGS YOU CAN DO WITH A USELESS MAN
MORE THINGS YOU CAN DO WITH A USELESS MAN
THE WORLD'S GREATEST PUT-DOWN LINES
LITTLE INSTRUCTION BOOK OF THE RICH & FAMOUS
WELCOME TO YOUR MIDLIFE CRISIS
GETTING EVEN WITH THE ANSWERING MACHINE
ARE YOU A SPORTS NUT?
MEN ARE PIGS / WOMEN ARE BITCHES

ARE WE DYSFUNCTIONAL YET?
TECHNOLOGY BYTES!
50 WAYS TO HUSTLE YOUR FRIENDS ($5.99)
HORMONES FROM HELL
HUSBANDS FROM HELL
KILLER BRAS & Other Hazards Of The 50's
IT'S BETTER TO BE OVER THE HILL THAN UNDER IT
HOW TO REALLY PARTY!!!
WORK SUCKS!
THE PEOPLE WATCHER'S FIELD GUIDE
THE UNOFFICIAL WOMEN'S DIVORCE GUIDE
THE ABSOLUTE LAST CHANCE DIET BOOK
FOR MEN ONLY (How To Survive Marriage)
THE UGLY TRUTH ABOUT MEN
NEVER A DULL CARD
RED HOT MONOGAMY
   (In Just 60 Seconds A Day) ($6.95)
HOW TO SURVIVE A JEWISH MOTHER ($6.95)
WHY MEN DON'T HAVE A CLUE ($7.99)
LADIES, START YOUR ENGINES! ($7.99)

Retail $3.95
NO HANG-UPS
NO HANG-UPS II
NO HANG-UPS III
HOW TO SUCCEED IN SINGLES BARS
HOW TO GET EVEN WITH YOUR EXES
TOTALLY OUTRAGEOUS BUMPER-SNICKERS ($2.95)

NO HANG-UPS – CASSETTES Retail $4.98
Vol. I: GENERAL MESSAGES (Female)
Vol. I: GENERAL MESSAGES (Male)
Vol. II: BUSINESS MESSAGES (Female)
Vol. II: BUSINESS MESSAGES (Male)
Vol. III: 'R' RATED MESSAGES (Female)
Vol. III: 'R' RATED MESSAGES (Male)
Vol. IV: SOUND EFFECTS ONLY
Vol. V: CELEBRI-TEASE